Pa

The Singing and Dancing

Acknowledgements

Thanks are due to the editors of the following publications in which some of the uncollected poems first appeared: *The Nerve: The 1998 Virago Book of Writing Women*, *Staple*, *Writing Women*.

'Luminary' was commissioned by Derbyshire County Council and launched at Buxton Museum and Art Gallery to celebrate their exhibition 'Faces in the Crowd: Joseph Wright and Friends in Georgian Derbyshire'.

'Feretting' is from a sequence of poems commissioned by the Bakewell Show and Arts in the Peak during Ann's tenure as Poet Laureate of the Peak.

'Shot Put' was inspired by Yasmin Spencer, the Women's Youth Shot Put No.1 in 2010. It was commissioned by Derbyshire County Council for the Cultural Olympiad. Published on posters and postcards, it also appeared in *Let's Play! Poems About Sports and Games* (Frances Lincoln 2013).

Previous publications from which the present collection has been drawn: *Take Five* (Shoestring Press 2003), *Drawing Water* (smith|doorstop 2009), *From Matlock to Mamelodi: 5,000 Miles of Poetry with the Derbyshire Poet Laureate Ann Atkinson* (Derbyshire County Council 2011).

The Singing and Dancing:
Collected Poems

Ann Atkinson

smith|doorstop

Published 2015 by
smith|doorstop books
The Poetry Business
Bank Street Arts
32-40 Bank Street
Sheffield S1 2DS
www.poetrybusiness.co.uk

ISBN 978-1-910367-39-1 paper
ISBN 978-1-910367-57-5 cloth

British Library Cataloguing-in-Publication Data.
A catalogue record for this book is available from the
British Library.

Typeset by Utter
Printed by Lightning Source
Cover design by Utter
Cover image 'Hood Brook' by Victoria Hill, used by kind
permission of the artist.
Companion Stone photo by Holly Atkinson

smith|doorstop Books is a member of Inpress,
www.inpressbooks.co.uk. Distributed by Central Books Ltd.,
99 Wallis Road, London E9 5LN.

The Poetry Business is an Arts Council
National Portfolio Organisation

Contents

from *Take Five (2003)*

Drawing Water (2009)

from *From Matlock to Mamelodi (2011)*

For Lucas and Flynn

Foreword

In the 1970s Don Measham of Matlock College and his colleagues organised a series of Writers' Weekends, chiefly for the benefit of alumni of the college teaching locally and others associated with the college; they also attracted groups from as far north as York and as far south as Leicester. Each weekend featured one of the college's succession of Writers in Residence, always fiction writers – the Yorkshire novelists Stan Barstow and Barry Hines and the peripatetic-cum-vagrant Jack Trevor Storey: I was on hand to take some of the poetry workshops. Ann was a spirited member of these groups and that was our first meeting. We quickly struck up what was to prove an enduring and untroubled friendship. After one particularly productive weekend the college launched the magazine *Staple*, which Ann was later to co-edit. The magazine soon established a poetry competition, and I was asked to judge the anonymously-submitted entries. When the writers came to be identified I found I had awarded one of the prizes to Ann – for lucidity.

This was no random opinion. Poetry for Ann was a currency, like conversation, its nature being to capture and clarify elusive ideas that might otherwise remain unformed: so her characteristic style was natural and conversational, often with a crackle of verbal play, and an alertness to the possibilities of language that enabled her to achieve an effect of sensuous exuberance without becoming incoherent or merely fancy. I believe she had an innate sense of composition. She was a pianist and a skilled listener to music, with a background in dance and an openness to visual art and design. In poetry she had an enviable talent for beginning a piece without ceremony and ending it without strain: not every poet can do both. She was a very good writer.

The secure and even tone was not echoed in her material, for her poetry had no core preoccupations or obsessions. There were no apparent limits to her curiosity and observation about the world or her inner experiences; and it may be that the easy-going tone made it possible for her to work comfortably in various directions. Fluency, artistic confidence across an already-wide range of interests and a willingness to make something out of unpromising material made her an ideal recipient for the commissions that came her way, even when the invitations set challenges that stretched her imagination by taking her into subject matter she found bizarre. Most of the commissions were generated locally, something she found particularly satisfying, since it chimed with her conviction that poetry was capable of finding its own ways of by-passing socially-induced boundaries. This had been one of the assumptions behind the Matlock weekends.

Ann loved being in the company of writers: established figures, long-term practitioners or complete beginners. She was in her element wherever poetry was being made, and she made little or no distinction between the roles she took in a variety of situations: as tutor to a university class; as one of a small random gathering at an Arvon Foundation retreat; as convenor of a self-supporting writing holiday in a house she'd rented for the purpose; as guiding spirit to an ad hoc collection of her interested neighbours. Totally devoid (though she did lead an eventful life) of the self-fixation that seems to motivate many poets, she was able to teach without being dominant or prescriptive and to appear as a natural and unassuming character in her own poems.

For years it had seemed incongruous that she had no book-length collection. There was certainly enough work for a satisfying volume which would have made her writing more widely known and discussed; but in the face of constant nagging from friends and supporters she continually avoided the issue in words to the effect that yes, the collection was in existence but she herself didn't feel ready to see it published. She held both of Derbyshire's two laureateships in succession and during those years people became accustomed to hearing mainly about her public writings and activities; but the compilers of the present collection were surprised to discover how large a proportion of her completed but unpublished work had apparently been written in what I think of as a traditional way – in solitude. Much of this work is included here and will extend the experience of those fortunate enough to have known this remarkable woman; new readers will be bound to come face to face with her somewhere in these pages.

> – Roy Fisher
> January 2015

Introduction

As Ann's daughters, we are so proud to present this collection of our remarkable mum's work. Together with mum's friends and fellow poets River Wolton, Jim Caruth and Sally Goldsmith, we have gathered this collection together by searching her computer, her published work and asking friends and fellow writers to send us any versions they had. It is a difficult task to edit the poems of someone whose work you know and love but who isn't here to help guide the process. The job of an editor is usually to cut and improve but in these circumstances our task was to collect and order. We haven't altered her poems but we haven't included any that seemed unfinished; we also left out some commissioned poems that lost strength when taken from the context in which they were written. Where there were many drafts of a poem it was down to a collective editorial decision on which to include. Where published poems were later revised, we have used the most recent versions. The collection ranges from her first published poem, 'Late', through her several pamphlets and anthologised work to the manuscript she had put together in the autumn prior to her death. The title of the latter was *The Singing and Dancing* and we have kept it as the title of this book.

This is a large collection of published and unpublished poems. If anyone questions the poems we have selected and the way we have presented it, we can only say that everything was done out of love and admiration for this exceptional poet. For us it is not only a collection of poetry, it is a map of our lives, our experiences, and the history of our family, all told in our mum's distinctive and familiar voice. There is so much joy and warmth in these poems, and so many memories. We hope you enjoy reading them.

– Holly Atkinson
– Rosie Dymond

Early Uncollected Poems (1984 –2005)

The New Piano
for Lol and Rya Wharton

The old one fitted like a glove,
finger worn, nail scratched at the backboard
where Dad played *You'll never know
just how much I love you,* the broad span
of the major chords vamped
up and down the black notes,
and the flakes of varnish black
as the shipyard muck under his hard as nails nails.

And Mam's soft whistle somehow echoed
in the strings from her duster's arpeggios.
Before TV. Christmas time. The songs.

Me practicing Mozart, a tentative touch,
but growing, finding the pattern, the code
until it flowed, and Mam whistled Mozart
through her breathy lips, and Dad hummed
and tapped the rhythms on the arm of the chair.

To say the old piano rang with all of that.

But then, the heating cracked the soundboard,
dried its felts and hammers till it sounded bad.
So I bought the new one, with the money
that you left. A Yamaha, no inlaid mother of pearl,
just simple, and shining black as a coffin.

And I'm playing like you never heard, like
you'll never know, flying up and down
these easy keys, the light touch of it.

Here and There – with Schrödinger and Pavlov

(Both Cat and Dog had run away, alarmed
by boxes and exasperated by the bells.
Cat said, sometimes hers had looked

straight through her till she felt
she'd fall apart. Dog said, his kept
making promises that came to nothing,

that he was sick of being led on. And
so they met, and rubbed along. Dog
didn't like the little bell Cat wore.)

It was text book, my emergency stop,
the training had paid off, but sad
about the cat. It brought me round,

the shock. I'd driven over twenty miles
and no idea how, where I had been.
Last thing I registered, that strange

unfastened feeling, was I'd not put on
my watch. (I always leave it on the table
but I'd swear it wasn't there this time.)

Then from there to the here and now.
Your letter came that morning.
That's where I'd been, with you. Revisited

the best times, and the worst. I know this,
when I saw you, I became myself. It was
like that, a song, across a crowded room,

and ever since. That's where I'd been
for twenty miles, and then the cat.
(An old man brought a box out for the cat.)

A dog paced. Then streets away an ambulance
rings out. The dog sits, whimpers. That night
the phone call gets us nowhere, you saying

I'd not seen you as you really were, me
shouting, trying to make you see.
Next day I drive a different route,

streets away from where I killed the cat.
There are flowers on a telegraph pole,
one bouquet for somebody's dog, the rest

for the driver who had died, and had my name.
Red roses, tied to a pole. The message
from her lover saying, love (nothing) is forever.

The Woman Mistaken for a Hat

His pictures hang chronologically. Observe
Doctor, the strange development of vision.
Once he could paint as well as he could sing.
From what was real, to focus between edge
and negative, then interplay of hand, brush,
colour uncontained, agnosia of form. *See.*
Here he began to look at sound.

In the garden she becomes a tree which speaks
to offer him a rose. *What is this?*
A green of sharps, a form of convoluted red
which lacks platonic solid symmetry. Smell it
and he sings – Die Rose, Die Lilie, dum de dum –
and picks his way into a house, remembering.

Common nouns are guessing games. Is shoe
like foot a key for floor, a wife more hat
than head. Music shapes his order now.
At this space where sky is framed he hears,
conducts a counterpoint of traffic and the sound
of distant trains, the storm that clamours, shaking
his hypothesis of house, a scherzo furioso.

Silent, I am an absence for hours. Sitting,
I am chair, sleeping I am bed. Stand still
and I'm the clock that needs reminding to tick.
My shape shifts to insignificance. The hand,
the food I offer, one, unless I say –
this is food. Sing. Eat. You recommend
Doctor, that he makes his life entirely
of music? If only I could sing.

She prompts mnemonics for the lines
he moves along, speaks her face into his spaces,
punctuates the bars in common time of dressing,
bathing, eating. He will accompany each score,
hum-de-hum melodiously of commonplace.
Lately, I have taken to waiting in the hall,
by the hat stand, by the door.

Revisiting Crackendale
(for D.M.H.)

How the fields knew your tread,
even dark stones,
the way kept thin by your remembering.

How each gate drew your hand, welcome
to know its latch again,
familiar, your scent, fox hair on fence wire.

The wall opened up to let you through
and echoes were ready for your step.
They waited for you,

in the candle, its wax flow set, waited
in the rust of the hinge, the scrape of grit.
The house is turning to earth.

There are its women who died on the green road
lost in the white-out. There is the wife picking flowers
for her husband still dead upstairs.

Pick feverfew and camomile from the cracked yard,
leave them at the window.
The candle is burned out. Go.

The path away is a long dark and the stars are blurred.
Slip your hand in your pocket, there is a ghost hand
waiting. Take its comfort.

When Ted Hughes Died

I remembered the first years of my children's lives
in the high field above Eyam. The two-mile
in-all-weathers walk when the old car was junked
at the end of our lane. The wreck of it,

simmering in its oils, the acid ticking
its quick oxidations. The crash in the night
when lads from the village took its wheels
and dropped it off the jack, which they also pinched.

I remembered it heaped on the lane, over months
how the ground reached into the wreck,
the chassis wound with ragwort, dock, its pipes
throttled, so that when we had it winched away

its fluids drained into the wrench of pale growth,
the shape marked out in oil and rust,
and I knew that left to its own, the earth
would have had it back whole.

I remembered the years we lived raw in that field,
my feral children awake at dawn, striding out
half naked to count chickens, collect eggs.
My dreams were alert, so I'd wake knowing

where the good hen laid away, that that day
the sheep would lamb, then hold my children quiet
while the silver caul steamed out of the ewe
and she freed her lamb to the air.

I remembered the spring when they unearthed
their lost toy, its colour leached out
into layers of peat, and a bantam chick squawked
at a mole's snout earthing up, and a family

of wrens flew in and as fast out of the kitchen
stopping my breath. And while I was still
his voice was there on the radio, amazing me,
that the poems he read understood my hillside field

and entered my heart, as the machinery of grass
claims a child's toy, a car, takes it back to the earth.

The Coincidence of Sky

All day we watched the sycamore's
dismemberment. The men climbed

like boys with a plan. Balancing
out on a limb, with single-handed

chainsaws, they cut
the ground from underneath their feet.

And all day more and more sky
slid into the space the tree

was leaving. The tree grew taller
with each amputation (its hydraulics

rattled with airlocks) till it was stark
and high as an osprey's roost, and smoke

from the kindling pile rose.
On the same day, she had flown

to the coast, and phoned to say,
look up at the sky at five and wave.

At five we listened for a small engine
above the snarl of chainsaws, scanned

the sky till it came, pin-silver,
over the valley trees and closer,

dipping over the pitch of the roof.
Look mother. Look grandmother. Look,

I'm flying. We waved from the garden,
dancing, the dog leaping, barking.

And as she circled, we followed, spun
round to the tree as the loudest sound

was a splintering rage and a groan
as the sycamore fell, and the plane

flew through the space where it had been.
She filmed us from the plane.

There's a small blue figure dancing,
an old woman watching, a drift of smoke.

Cow

I watch the calf curve his neck up
and lift a long tongue curled to the udder.
The cow stands, halted, closes her eyes
slowly, like a woman caressed.

I feel the calf's long pulling
contract hard between navel and cervix,
recall, when Rosie cried out, hungry
spasms soaked my dress with sweet spilled milk
the stillness of my breast in her mouth
her small tongue pulling.

Then I wore my dress loose to slip easy
with my mother's tongue I licked her hands clean
bit her soft nails short. Remembered
how my grandmother with my head held firm
licked the lash out of my stinging eye.

The cow waits, wary at my watching
wipes a green tongue round her calf's milky mouth
begins to chew again.

Now my dress is fastened tight, my nature dry
folded, neat, like a pure white nightgown
my grandmother kept in a drawer to be buried in.

An Itch in the Palm

A shriek from the bathroom.
My daughter's bent over the bath drain,
tugging at a fibrous clog.

Another yank, a plug of matted hair
big as a small rat splurges out,
a dark sinuous tail trailing.

That hair belongs to none of us,
but easy to name her friends who've stayed
and bathed, luxuriating in the length

and depth of our old bath, those friends
with long dark hair, leaving us
this stomach-heaving souvenir.

The hair-rat's gone,
the flouch pure vortex,
the drain, clean.

The night before this in a dream,
I'd picked at a sore, an itch
in the palm of my hand.

My mother says, an itch on the right's
for getting, the left, for parting with.
And there at the end of the line

for my heart, a spelk end, a thread
at its point of entry. I tug at it,
pull, and draw out the inches of hair,

a long fair daughter-hair, leaving sore
red lines in my palm where it had nested.
The lines that apparently map my life.

A Small Red Car

She watched from the car
as the plane took off
        I saw a small red car
        as the plane banked
she watched the plane
climb out over the sea
        it was a toy car
        she, a child waving
for her, my leaving was a plane
growing small over the ocean
        the ache of leaving's fixed
        on the small red car, disappearing

Flying Home

the hours lost going
are given back as the longest dawn
burning off the red Arabian cloud.
Unveiled, the horizon arcs sharper
in my fisheye. Miles up, the circle's smaller.

From Mount Terrangowan
we'd caught the tail-end of the comet,
a dim flare. But the stars are different there,
the geometry of the Southern Cross,
the calculation of due south evaded me.

At home, the stars have their sky
that these hills each night roll past.
Still the ground's unsteady.
The comet's gone out on its tangent.
We are abandoned.

Not Christmas

I wrapped her gifts for airmail.
Contents of parcel: dog hair,
house dust, wood smoke, and cells
of my skin peeled on the sellotape:
the with love messages
she would not read for weeks.

Christmas Eve. Eleven hours ahead,
she'll wake to the bright sun
one hundred and sixty degrees
before our morning dawns.
We'll glimpse the same sun low
and thin, that scorched her skin,
a world's half turn ago.

Christmas. We mark time
till she's home again. One thing
is constant: the way our lives connect,
our molecules spin, will share the rush
and sway of blood until mine stills.
And even then.

*

Months after she'd gone, the comet
hauled over our valley, its tail a lit wake,
its pathway west, though west
from such a distance had no meaning.
The sighting from the world's far side
was not so clear she said. I juggled
oranges and tried to understand
trajectories, could barely grasp
the principle of how we spin in space.

Come Spring, I'd bought my ticket.
Would spend my fiftieth year
on the other side of this world.

Reptile Picture-Postcards from Australia

Uluru

We are ingrained with red dust.
It has rained, the spinifex has flowered
and our skin creeps with flies.
A thorny devil, tiny dinosaur,
edges like a wind-up toy
into the blue scrub shade.

Camp Crocodilus

The rainforest air is a green salve.
A Boyd's lizard grasps a sapling piccabeen,
rotates each independent eye.
On the forest floor a leaf-tailed gecko
stills in the torch beam, thinks
of merging in a mulch of leaves.

Cape Tribulation

The air's burned dry, the white sand tracked
to burrows under the coconut palms.
We're tacky with sun-block, salt.
By the information board, a lace monitor
stretches its olive stencilled length
beneath a picture of itself.

Fitzroy Island

The goanna is shredding its parchment skin,
its tongue tastes six inches of our scent, and turns
a yard-long drag carving the sand.
On the coral path, an odd length of hose
snatches moonlight into a hiss and snakes off.
In our bunkroom the geckos cheep like birds
scuttle after spiders, their fingers suckered onto glass.

Cairns (Duane Cash, Skin Art)

A sting of deliberate serrations, the dab
and blot of running ink, blood,
the fine line of lizard under my skin.

Dive Boat – Cairns

We gather knots out of Trinity Dock.
Land shrinks in the wake: level is lost,
the sea busy with the wind, jigging the horizon.

Moored at Norman Reef and seal-skinned
I gaze to the horizon, turn, and turn
to realise the ocean's circle, me at its centre.

Ease myself down and in,
and goggle-eyed, gape at what is under,
me, floating above the reef's canopy –

each time I tell it, the word for fish
is birds, for reef, tree, the giant wrasse
a cow's bulk that nuzzles at my ghostly hands.

And then, the reef falling away, fathomless,
to have no substance, weightless, a heart-lurch
flying with the beautiful birds.

One day at sea, two days before the fluid
in my ears calms. My dreams swim with the fish,
the ground awake shifts under my feet.

Port Douglas: The Last Day

A fair, music and jugglers, as night falls
we walk along the beach.

Bats trawl the floodlights by the swimming nets:
the sea is syrup edged with moon:

the jugglers play with fire – arcs of torches
round the campers' barbie fires.

In the morning, the hired car,
the air-conditioned airport.

A Long Story

A two-foot fish on the slab
by the garden tap, the jelly-eyed gape

of slack muscle. Jean-Paul flaps the tail,
swims it gawping at his little son who squeals

across the lawn towards Monique, who has ushered
the English couple through the brown hush

of the shuttered house into the garden.
(The woman's discomfort – the casual invitation –

drunk at Le Dinosaur Bistro, and Frank's insistence,
of course they'd be welcome). His school French,

Elle n'aimez pas le soleil, explains her seat in the shade,
loose dress, pale skin. Ricard – a sickly taste of aniseed.

Monique wears a white bikini.
Jean-Paul strokes her brown skin, her flat belly.

Monique's mother wears black, from headscarf
to espadrilles, has come with a knife

for the fish, gestures
with its point to her watch, then to the guests.

Frank is oblivious, rattles the ice in his glass.
Monique's mother scrapes at the fish.

The rasping wrong-way sound. Scales glint
in the sun, catch in her hair's frizz, sequin

her dress, arms, face. The thought
of the fish scales catch in the throat,

the gag.(Her distaste even now, for aniseed.)
They are told it is time to leave,

Monique's English polite, precise.
(The son must be thirty now, at least.)

She remembers the day after that, her trying
to get a tan, Frank, in flippers and mask, swimming

off Les Sables d'Olonne and gone too long.
The fuss of the lifeguards hauling him in

from the off-shore current.
What if they hadn't.

Three-Toed Sloth

You will observe I am solitary. I breathe,
eat and sleep tree. Though apparently myopic
I know a thousand ways for leaves to filter light.
In each long sleep I dream as tree

and undisturbed, my algae grow me green.
I wake to the hatch of moth-eggs, the graze
of larvae worming my leaves. I am adorned
by chrysalides and feel the ease of becoming.

My suckling young learn rising sap from me;
leave us, or I'll aim a felling blow
and carve my clawed toes deep as bone.
Each year in a reflection of tree-shade, sky,

I swim the forest river to the other side.
My fact is that I carry tree. A transient crawl
on heavy ground, then reinstated and confirmed
I hang fresh rain in my familiar canopy.

The Painter who lives with the Netsuke Carver

the only view is his. he finds the grain
in the mammoth's tusk, the torque
to hold the moment of the mantis,
its grip before the bite.

his concentration's laser keen.
the room is red with it.
if his blade slips a millionth
there'll be hell to pay. tiptoe.
close the door without a sound.
don't open the fridge, disturb the larvae
he's trawled the river for. do without milk.

her canvas stretches, waits for her to put a foot wrong ...
god knows he's tutored her. there's nothing
he doesn't know of texture, line, but will she learn.
she's a landscape's sweep of wasted paint.

under the microscope the larvae squirm,
through the lens, the tracery of a damselfly,
the wings that he will replicate in bone.
he will drill until the nerve's exposed.
so skin is glass. he says: listen to me,
I am patience, the metaphor
for all the grains of sand. trust me.

Delicacy

There was a fat moth in the left-over
Vegetables a la Greque, stained
russet in the tomato sauce. A chance

landing while the dish had cooled might
have bogged its legs in. These legs
were up, stiff, all six, pale gold

and cooked. We'd dined by candlelight.
I don't know how I'd not dished up
the sticky corpse onto his plate.

Years ago, by the BBC's light flicker
my father, eating supper (crackers, pickle,
cheese) bit into a moth and retched

loudly, coughing food and moth and both
sets of teeth into his hands, dashed out
to vomit in the kitchen sink. Afterwards

the programme we were watching lost
its thread, him raking up at intervals and
spitting sizzling gobs into the fire.

Moths dive at me as though my face
were lit. I can't rest till they're caught,
shudder at dust on my palms, the hook

of their feet. I did not tell the guest
about the one he'd missed. The chance
moth in the mouth. The indelicacy.

Found Twin

I conjured her. Before her image formed
all other days had been unedged, low lit

like Januaries. Nights lipped on the hills.
Each day hauled yesterday with its dawn –

the smell of stale bread, indents on cushions –
and in the ashy grate, wafers of burned pages,

words only a shimmer on the paper's ghost.
And forced white tulips craned

pale stems to the light and dropped their petals
like stilled tongues on the windowsill.

She was always somewhere. I closed my eyes
and saw her in the halo of a reading lamp

turning the quiet pages of her book.
I took my time bringing her close.

Located now, she occupies the moment.
I know the way dusk settles on her house,

brings badgers to her door. She has charmed
the roe deer from the woods. She sings with owls.

There is no question. She regulates my days.
She is a hazy light, sun on her bent back.

I bring her to mind, and hers is my image
by which I am witnessed. She lets me be.

Should she stop for a moment, she can,
should she choose to, conjure me.

Becoming Mary: Becoming Myra

So it begins: it begins so gentle
and from the heart. Mother, father,
entangled in the broth and swelter.
In the wrestle and throb, spilt then
and immersed, united: simmered,
then split and untied, as DNA repeats, *I.*
is separate, and one miracle: assign *Us.*
A ceremonial sings *Us,* as each
cell replaces itself, as each cell
self-replicates our platonic symmetry,
our compliant mystery. Here, we trace
in detail. There, we are identical.
A meaning is rescued, an enigma
is secured. Become my tender name Myra
Become Mary my endearment.

So it begins
gentle and from the heart.
In the broth and swelter,
spilt then, and immersed, united
as DNA repeats *I.*
One miracle: assign *Us,*
as each cell replaces itself,
our platonic symmetry.
Here we trace in detail:
a meaning is rescued.
Become my tender name Myra.

It begins so:
mother, father, entangled
in the wrestle and throb:
simmered, then split and untied,
is separate, and
a ceremonial sings *Us*
as each cell self-replicates
our compliant mystery.
There we are, identical:
an enigma is secured.
Become Mary my endearment.

Monozygotic twins have identical DNA, and the 'language of genes' has a simple
alphabet – only 4 letters, A G C T, the initial of each of the four amino acids, adenine,
guanine, cytosine and thymine which join in variations of groups of 3 to make
proteins, the building blocks of the body. This poem consists of anagrams, and plays
with the idea of a limited stock of letters producing similar but individual meanings.

Late

In the busyness and bloody relief of my birth
someone forgot, while checking my heart, to whisper,
This is it, start living now.
And later, warmed and accustomed to the noise and light,
I waited, but they assumed I knew.

My father worked overtime, time after time and a half
so we could start to live.
And I marked time and said, *When I grow up I'll be.*

Not long before his worn out end of time
my father clutched the last and shortest straw
and said, *When I retire I'll take my time, relax and live.*

And I, biding my time,
waiting for my real life to begin,
said, *When I am free I'll be.*

Then in the busyness and bloody relief of his death
did someone forget, while checking his heart, to whisper,
That was all.
And later, cold and accustomed to the quiet and dark,
he thrust me late and frantic into life.

Bathroom with Glass Door

The glass is reeded. The image
multiple, cut to the raw.

✳

He left the door wide open.
The child crept close, gazed
up between his straddled legs.
What spout, what torrent's roar,
just as he turned to see her there.

The children bathe. A new flat loofah
swells and sheds black seeds. What mystery
of brother. She picks seeds from her skin
and keeps them safe, clutching at her towel.

✳

His shaving soap was in a tube.
The cream was scented, palest green.
She loved its shimmer, could not resist
to squeeze a little, and a little more
until it came and came in pearly
wormcast whorls onto her palm.

✳

Blood spreads in the white foam
on his neck. He shouts. Her hands
silk up her guilty legs.

*

Sun prints leaf shadows on the green
gloss walls. She sinks into steam.
Soap. Oil. Lush. Lush. A cool spring
licks her feet. And drains.
She leaves the bathroom clean.

*

Twelve years since he died and still
his razor, soap and brush sit on your shelf
set in their venus scallop shell.

Each time I see them there, I know,
and gently rock that shell to shift
his dust, and glimpse again

his tender shaving of your hair,
a towel held beneath your upraised arm,
before the door discreetly closed.

Mother, about the Corner China Cabinet ...

it was a white lie, the tactful *yes,*
I'll have it when you die. But then you did
and I had to keep my word.

For years it's been out of place,
and full of itself, its mirrors
kaleidoscoping your bits of glass and pot.

And if I reach in, peer sideways to catch
my elusive face, there's a carousel of hands
like yours, the clatter of glass on glass.

Today, a friend told me how a clairvoyant
saw the details of her life, reeled off names,
events, her long-dead father's wink and nod.

She was convinced. But I hesitate
to write this, forgive me, we both know
you never believed that stuff.

Like when that gypsy fortune teller
pressed a glass bead in my palm for luck
and stung me for a fiver, you tapped your foot

and pulled the purse-strings of your lips,
and the gypsy tipped her head, said
don't worry about that one, she'll be alright.

And I think you will. Don't read these words:
that the moment you died and I pressed my hands
to your chest something in me changed. And since,

I'm full of the pleasing of you, so sometimes
it's you who opens my mouth or who shuts it,
who opens my eyes, looks back from the mirror.

Don't watch when I pack all the keepsakes,
dispose of the cabinet; don't take it to heart.
It's been good and odd to have you, but it's time
you moved out. I'll be fine on my own.

Just the Pattern of the Streets

for Honora Barber nee Jones

Over there, where children race on bikes
around the pattern of the streets, that
was Osborne Street. Just thirty-two
running steps from our door to my Gran's.
I could make a cry last that long,
my blonde plaits thudding on my back
till I plunged into her arms for comfort.
There was her yard where the distempered lav
smelled of the sage and mint she'd hung to dry.

The school will soon be gone.
Through fallen plaster and broken glass,
still the smell of school, chalk-dust and ink,
charcoal, children. Here a hoard of compositions
has spilled from a cupboard like a looted barrow –
the new round writing, the names I recognise,
Clocherty, Crosswaite, Corcoran, Lowers.

I sat here, looked out to Tees Street
when this room was warm with the hum
of never-ending now: when launchings
meant time out of school, and shipyard
sirens measured out our days – until the day
when Dad had fallen forty feet and died.
All I could feel was the stroke of his thumb
when he'd held my hand that morning.

There is dust on my hands like ash.
Across the playground a girl watches me,
for a moment our eyes meet, and then
she runs away, and I can feel
the thud of her long plaits on my back.

51

Stonemason

A man outside my window chisels stone.
A rhythmic thudding, his lump-hammer strikes
the wooden butt, a force transmits from hand
through hand to cutting blade. A clear note rings

sings out, pure G. I press a key, hammer
to string, match the pitch of metal on stone,
play a chord, and improvise progressions
over his staccato theme. He pauses,

inspects the edges of the chiselled stone,
how far to cut before it fits the shape
he has in mind, then strikes again, just once.
The piano reverberates. I feel

the note, the chord. His rhythm's in my head.
The stone is cut, and bedded in the wall.

Opening Night

After the waiting
and all the rehearsing,
here, now, wired to gadgetry
that ticker tapes the rhythm
of my slow progress,
... such potions squeezed into
my rigged tubes,
that on my way to the theatre
I almost disappeared.

There in the spotlit centre
much waving and draping of green cloths
... now you see it, now you don't ...
bright steel flashing in the white light
and nothing up any sleeve.

A murmur from the crowd ...
the Indian woman enters, ready
a turquoise sari skirts her theatre gown
her red caste mark
a focus to hypnotise my eyes.

It begins.
A slow roll of drums.
... Ladies and gentlemen,
I shall now cut this woman in two ...
the drum roll louder
suspense and incantations
mumbled behind masks,
                    a hush
the moment comes, then a sound
like a wellington sucked out of a bog.

She lifts my shining child
high to the theatre lights
an offering to the gods
and the drums sound out
with trumpets and applause

and in that silence
I touched my child
and we were perfect.

Gap Year

If I could haul her back from there
when she turned at the barrier
to say *where do I go.*
But we had traced the route,
strung the continents with crosses.
Just follow the signs. Go on
to the other side of the world.

How could I eat or sleep,
but pace an empty house, wait
for the telephone, her voice
when it comes, through sweet teeth
and the line awash in a lake
deep enough for a swan to beat its feet on.

And if I don't sleep it's the wind
telling tales from the forest.
If I dream it's the thorns of roses,
a daisy kept in a box by a shepherd,
a secret in a locket.

Cast white sheets over the space.
Catch whatever moves.

All I can say is I waved her off
and it wasn't her came back –
she had flown with the swans,
the trail was lost, berries
to the birds, seeds to the wind.

All I know is it's too late
to spoon delicious food into her mouth.
Pinch the skin to see if we're dreaming,
say *give me your hand.* Feel the bone.

Nushu

Denied ink and the men's code of ideograms,
we dip our sharp bamboo in cook-pot soot
and sing our sound poems with our sisters,
for our daughters. Denied easy steps,
our songs dance on tiptoe up our pages,
arch like an unbound foot, a graceful hand,
each word a flower, a willow stitched into cloth,
painted on our silk fans, each phonogram
an open mouth the shape of our painted lips
and a finger's hush, a sweet and quiet longing.

This third-day book is a gift to a daughter,
songs to go with her into her marriage,
the songs women sang, sworn sister songs,
mother-love songs and the habit of singing
and the book is for filling, its pages are mirrors,
the book is a space to fill with her future,
to fill with her mournful songs, grace
with the flowing of secret songs,
songs she will teach to her daughters – this
is the book we will take to the grave with us.

Night Shift

Someone should watch the passing of the night,
time the slow turn of the constellations, witness
which way the river runs, the moon's phasing of the tide.

Someone should stay awake when the storm blows,
should hold the furniture in place, the carpets down,
check for power-cuts, that the fridge light still comes on.

Someone should keep the phone-lines clear for talking,
books on their shelves, words on the page for reading.
Someone should watch to keep us in our beds, and breathing.

The House

I can see myself here she said,
loving the window light, the way
it nurtured the air of the rooms
she knew from her dreams.

So she lives there, never surprised
by a glimpse of herself grown old,
in a chair by the fire, her sigh in the night,
fading into the walls.

If sometimes she yearns for the sea
and the home with a white shingle gate,
she stays, and says under her breath
be patient old woman. Wait.

Basil

I'm tearing the leaves
when you've only to brush them
and the kitchen's awash with the scent.
There's depth to this sauce,
tomatoes, garlic and rough red wine,
it catches my breath, tight in my throat,
sharp as our parting, salt as choked-back tears.
I'm back there then, all the way home on the train,
in my hands the pot of basil you'd grown – a gift,
the leaves, trembling tongues on their stems.
The smell was the whole train long.
Even after the journey, for hours
my hands smelled of it, my lips, my skin.

My hands smelled of it, my lips, my skin,
even after the journey, for hours.
The smell was the whole train long,
the leaves, trembling tongues on their stems,
in my hands, the pot of basil you'd grown – a gift.
I'm back there. Then all the way home on the train,
sharp as our parting, salt as choked-back tears,
it catches my breath, tight in my throat.
Tomatoes, garlic and rough red wine,
there's depth to this sauce
and the kitchen's awash with the scent.
When you've only to brush them
I'm tearing the leaves.

Twenty

The advice on giving up, was think
of every cigarette you've ever smoked
laid end to end, a chain, the load
you carry. Think of the damage, the tar
and stink. Drop it. Think of the weight
off your mind. Think of the trail we left
like markers to find a way home.

✳

I'd driven late to see you, had to sleep.
You're awake in the half light, watching
my eyes move. I'm watching the dream.
The dream is you're handing a note to me,
I'm reaching out taking it. Waking
is touching your hand, the taste of your lips.

✳

Travelling there's a need to draw breath,
mark the place, remember it all. Rest
And Be Thankful, the view into Hell's Glen,
ash scattering on the wind. Cross Fell,
sunlight blazing the Solway Firth.
Berlin. Coffee. After The Wall.

✳

By the hearth your brown dog twitches
in her dream of quick foxes. We hear
the clock's counting, must talk before
giving up on the day. Struck match,
a deep intake of breath, and the words
come visibly stuttering.

*

Or sitting on the rock in the bracken
talking of rabbits, my dog impatient.
Days after you'd gone, going back.
The evidence, leavings stubbed out
among droppings.

*

Another dark. A flint ignition, the sharp
of your face and cast shadows, a brief
illumination. And me in it, stroked
with fume and tongue, breathing
your intimate blown smoke.

*

We talk on the phone, late at night
when there's no other life but your voice
in my head. The flick and murmur
as you light another. Things not said.
When you speak you were thinking
of something else altogether.
Count the ends in my ashtray.

*

The pack's user-friendly, neat, a slick
strip of cellophane, thumb-flick lid,
easy-pull foil. I'm now so proficient
I can do it with one hand, in the dark,
in a pocket, while driving.

*

One thing I'd miss is this, the reliable
bowel regulation. That first smoke, the one
that coffee never tastes as good without,
is guaranteed to work. Imagine
the heart's rush flooding the system,
the quick peristalsis. Without it, a backlog,
distension. Rely on Lactulose, roughage,
the phone's sudden ring.

*

And the cough. When I laugh out loud
a tickle catches the trachea in spasm,
pleats intercostals. I read some statistic,
you can measure the tar in litres.
Some times, an ache under my breast
behind my ribs.

*

Burning, a cigarette has three thousand components.
My lungful's exhaled in a beam of sunlight, the smoke
from the tip's worth watching. There's carbon monoxide,
hydro-carbons, formaldehyde, amines and nitrosamines,
poisonous heavy metals – nickel, cadmium, arsenic,
lead. Breathe in. Out.

*

Whether it was toxins or the heart breaking,
that dispossession of the head. The stubbing out
and lighting up another, two hands shaking,
when you said that it was over.

*

The drag to take alone, comforter
of late nights, of hush and mood.
Whose red light lights my hand,
whose flare and sputter's close
as breath in my ear. Exhalations
count the slow beats of the night's
repetitions. The ash, disconsolation.

*

I caught sight of myself taking a drag.
Oh, the mouth's radial puckers, the pouch
filling under the chin. Not like a fifties' film,
no soft focus. All the lines are down.
What a mug's game. What a sucker.

*

I'd given up, my room was sweet. I changed
the linen, washed the curtains, polished,
vacuumed every trace. But when I pressed
my face into the pillow, missing you,
the smell was there still, deep.

*

Another lover. First time in my bed,
I didn't know whether my voice would sound
like mine when it said a different name, then
I saw you, smiling, your image fading by the door,
and I gasped. Like in a bad movie. So I lit a cigarette.

＊

Then the visit. Your place, there's
the evident other, the new, for better.
A photo of you she has taken and framed,
the colour, red, for the walls, you have chosen
together. Worse, her Ventolin at the side of the bed.

＊

A touching reunion. A cigarette rests
on an over-full ashtray. Catches.
Rekindles all the dead ends.

＊

The last one, with red wine.
A slow communion. Finish it.
The twentieth's saved, hidden.
A straw. A link. A possibility.

＊

＊

For Rosie on her Wedding Day

I remember this like yesterday –
you, two years old, and the rain,
days of it, that kept us in, until
I dressed you for the weather,
red wellies, zipped up waterproof,
and we ran in the downpour up the lane.

The rain was a river, so we made
a silver-paper boat to sail.
You let it go, and caught it up,
set it to sail again, and again.

Today, we have dressed you
for different weather, for your groom
who waits for you here.

And the gown that you wear
is the colour of sky after rain, blue-jade
as a warm sea to sail on, silk
that whispers like waves on a gentle shore.
And the sun, embroidered in leaf
and stem, like the gold of your hair.

Remember the small silver boat,
the walk to here on your father's arm,
for you were a gift to us, you are our joy.
Here's where the voyage begins
with your husband, with Chris,
who waits for you, patiently, now.

from *Take Five (2003)*

The Mozart Effect

Dr Franz Mesmer – 1768

I was entranced,
not by the silk and lace, the clever trickery,
but his hands' lucid dance on the clavier keys,
the exhilarating edge of seat pace,
his flight of wit.

It crossed my mind
to suggest he write a German operetta,
and delight surged in him, a theme
a melodic line, and variations
dancing in reply.

At my table, candlelight.
His father's chatter fades, the room
is circumscribed by light reflected in his eyes,
and when he looks at me, he fascinates.
I cannot look away.

October in my garden's open theatre,
the lanterns blur the stars and make a roof-vault
of the trees. He conducts: Bastien and Bastienne,
and the autumn's chill
turns into spring.

Then he was gone.
I have the manuscript written by his hand,
can trace his mind's progressions, its control,
and I'm distracted as the nights are long,
dangle my watch and chain

amazed by how slow the time.
I find I'm counting down the hours,
the days, the weeks since he has gone.
There is work to be done, I must
snap out of it.

Giles de la Tourette – 1855

Tourette's: the sudden intruder, the joker,
that trips the tongue to twitch and curse.
Giles made notes, observed grimace and tic,

and those who had learned
to turn the extravagance to good, improvise
tics to thrill, grimace to grace.

Mozart: his hands always busy, lacing the notes,
a tune to play, on the back of a chair, with a spoon,
a knife, tap it out with a pen, click the heels, count

the bars, the beats, tread the stairs running in triplets,
a glissando scale of banisters, the clatter of hoofbeats,
a sudden intrusion, a change of key – a skittish snatch

of petticoat, the flirt in the mirrored ballroom.
A million dominoes ready to fall at a push, a furl
and clack of keys, reflected, augmented, on and on.

Special School, Aberdare, 1999

We welcome them in from Merthyr Tydfil,
by bus, by taxi, from Hirwaun, Treorchy.
This is the school that will change the mind
of the school-refuser, the ruction-maker.
We aim to open up new horizons,
to change the tune of the don't-miss-a-tricker.
Here we look lively, talk tidy, sit up, take notice.
It's Mozart does it, soothes the restless agitation.
We've loudspeakers in corridors, classrooms –
opera, concerti, sonatas – here we listen to reason,
it's healing, a tonic, like a charming ECT.

They're coming at last to their senses
and go home fired, bright as the Brecon Beacons
watching over The Valleys, over the open-cast scars
of Hirwaun, the seamless repairs, the seeding of tips,
and the Mining Heritage Centre,
the smart big-shed factories, Sony, Hitachi.

Lady-Hares in a Forest

Over the phone she says,
Are you closing your eyes?

So am I. And we try with the mind's
eye to see the shape an arm

feels, the spread of a hand.
So each hand unravels its plan,

broadly spatulate, sparking as the image
thinks of touch.

As we had, at the gallery,
touched the woman-hare forms ravelled

in the sculptor's hands, us
small among them looking up into the face

of hare, the billowing ears
which think of Sophie's hair,

its massed curl, the form she used,
through which air moves

and a splintering light. We touched
the finger tips, cupped

the hands, and shrill
as owl call, the tangle of capillaries,

a tree's exposed nerve, became
our form. Still stripped of skin

we grazed our meal – succory
leaves, pine kernels, tomatoes small as berries

from the forest – drank cool wine,
and eased back into our same skin.

Over the phone, our eyes shut, her voice
ignites bright pixels that dance,

reaching out like a phantom limb
to complete the circuit, her hand, mine.

Lady-Hares in a Forest – Wire Sculpture, Sophie Ryder. Victoria Gallery, Bath, 1999

Of the Tropics

Colombo airport, Sri Lanka,
my first breath is spiced mildew.

Under the stairs, my father's kit-bag,
petty-officer's hat, long white socks.

Outside, the heat's slap and glare,
an avenue of fan-palms dancing.

Old photos. Him with the Tamil rick-shaw boy,
him posed with cross-armed men, the pale one

among snow-falls of flowers, his signature
fading. Forever Yours. From the monochrome,

he's breathing this air, skin freckled gold
and the orchids colour-washed in.

Over fifty years ago, and twenty of them dead,
and he's here to meet me in the flesh.

❋

Cape Tribulation. Night loud in the rain forest
and the ceiling fan's on *slow*. The rhythm turns

familiar, something like a name repeated, or a song
loosening my mind with memory that can't be mine,

knowing the smell of heat, the way clothes cling.
How as a child I told them when they asked that rice grows

in paddy fields, the water terraces, more, the ooze of mud
between the toes, green sharps breaking the waterskin.

At the Pennines' edge, high above Penistone,
the wind-farm turbines turn the sky about.

Lulled, I slow the car, listen. *My mother's name,
Rya, soft in his voice like a song, Rya.*

An ad on TV, a helicopter, film slowed down,
the rotor blades' pulse, hypnotic. I'm falling back.

A child in a white cotton dress. I know the verandah
where I am, because of the bicycle propped by the rail,

the view, low bushes where women twist off shoots of tea,
a train-track beyond. Dark inside the bungalow, a fan turning.

✳

Had I forgotten that he told me stories, remember
only knowing. I ask my mother, she is saying

*that was Ceylon, yes, that night he came back,
the smell on his clothes, on his skin.*

Far away for a moment, her name a song, *Rya, my Rya.
I fell with you, soon after he came home.*

He left Ceylon in July monsoon rains. I'm born in May,
late snow, some trace of the Tropics growing in me.

Fever Hospital: 1950

The bed grows bars, and hot.
I am a monstrous head on tiny limbs,
fin hands, fish tail, and the room
swims in my minnowing sleep.

My dark head is the room
they haul me from, and my mouth
is chalk. After the crisis I am cool,
watch from behind my eyes.

At home they give me a doll
whose eyes clatter open and shut.
Each night in my bed, the heat
swarms from my blood to her chill.

I bathe her, warm her by the fire,
until her seams begin to split and gape,
and I see the cat's-cradle sinews,
the lead weights of her eyes.

The nightmare, that my own head
cracks in two, I wake from,
my hands holding together
the two shells of my skull.

Henrietta Lacks: the HeLa Cell Line: 1954

Old Magic: a soul stolen
by a camera's flash, power
claimed with snips of finger nail,

a lock of hair. They were welcome
to their harvest from her cancer,
Henrietta was beyond all that.

A strange brew: chicken plasma,
serum of human placental cord, extract
of bovine embryo: a nutrient broth

on which her cells would thrive
and thrive. Even now, on petri dishes,
slides, in tissue banks, and stores

in pharms that work at modifiying DNA,
her cells continue to divide: a formless mass
of her, enough in bulk to populate a town,

each nucleus of every cell, the code
for her eyes, her hair, the way she danced,
her voice, the colours she preferred.

The Serpent's Tongue

I've bitten my tail long enough,
held my tongue. I tried to tell you
when I licked your ears, whispered

Look to the future, take a bite
of this, it's not forbidden.
(I'd tried it first, wormed into the core.)

I wished for more from you, the thirst
to understand the lovely spiral
of my zig-zag lacery, the chromosomal

message in my scales' silk braille.
You missed the point, got guilt.
I've squeezed between as many rocks

and places hard enough to slough
a million skins, while you wasted time
nurturing *The Lapse* out of your young.

At last you're listening, have learned
the programme's set that split second
sperm bites into egg. And now

you've cracked it, counted what the kit
consists of, mapped the bar-code string
that I epitomize. (Some had me down

for rainbows, carving valleys, the power
to move mountains. Some had my forked
tongue hiss with the devil. Jesus!) Listen,

I'm insistent, I'm the image of the one
and only Double-Helix God,
look, it's rippling along my spine.

Imagine, billions of miles, an eternity
of your DNA, enough to stretch
from here into another galaxy

and back again. You're in the nick
of time. Get picking out, eradicate
the sub, the ab, the retrograde. Be quick.

A whisper to the getting-wise:
the future's sleekly uniform,
symmetric, serpentine.

Surviving Twin

She is left-handed,
understands completely,

the elegance of numbers.
Division is second nature.

She talks to the mirror,
distracted, will turn

to find no-one watching her,
itch to catch the words

of a song on the tip
of someone else's tongue.

A dark mirror memory:
imprinted in each cell,

each molecule, as water
knows to run with water,

blood with blood,
the way a dance is fixed

by the choreography her limbs
have made. The counterbalance.

Ultra-sound images and high-speed scanners show twins as early as five weeks in one out of eight pregnancies. Only weeks later, the same test will show only singletons in all but one out of ninety pregnancies. Ten to fifteen percent of us are surviving twins. Professor Luigi Gedda, Gregor Mendel Institute, Rome, suggests that all left-handed people are survivors of vanished twin syndrome.

Surviving Conjoined Twin

I remain. a mirror
image of myself

learning to be
ambidextrous.

I am short of her breath
in my ear. the quiet.

my spirit levels
adjust vertical

and I am light-headed
deciding which way to go.

if I am half-hearted
it's her shadow haunts me.

trace the scar
map how we touched

thin skinned. kiss the mirror
miss her weight

The Teratology of Hisham Ragab's Twin

He kept it close for sixteen years, the whole
feeling of fullness, the strain in his back,

his side, till ache became pain, then acute.
The X-rays came as a shock. A dense sac tucked

near his kidney, a mass with spine and arm,
a head with a mouth, teeth, tongue.

Opinions divided. Teratoma – chaotic tissue
in a cyst big as a melon, or Hisham's twin,

division incompleted and adhered. Excision.
A seven-inch foetus, two kilos weight, alive.

Monstrous the not-named, never born. Only
a dark dream that was moist heat, and slide

of going, the run and flex of spine, loom
of fluid rhythm, and a voice drumming in him

stories of angles, lines, aridities of sand
and stone. Maybe the roll

of spices on his tongue, his open jaw.
His cry's a voice that Hisham hears in dreams.

His twin's a freak in a jar, shelved
with miracles and monsters, the unexplained.

Since January

I am no longer surprised. But the first glimpse
made me smile, the next few took my breath.

It's strange to see myself, and often driving
other people's cars. I catch my likeness

only in passing, and never eye to eye. I'm not
always this old. Last week I had long hair

and children in the back. I don't look for it.
It's always unawares, turning a corner, change

of the lights, when mine's on green, and brief,
but for that moment I am sure. I always smile.

I'd know my own smile anywhere.
You think of angels, but what with traffic

as it is today, the god on my dashboard's Janus,
the two-faced god of all our journeys, our comings

and goings, a god of beginnings. Like a god
who whittled at that boomerang bone and cast it

into the shape of Eve and Eve was born
again and again. Then January, a change:

in passing still, I looked right into my own
eyes, smile for smile, shock for shock.

Drawing Water (2009)

Then we drove on

but we had slowed at the same time,
stopped for the stoat on the road between us,
the still calf-lick of its alert, the poised streak
sleek away-through-the-hedge-and-gone of it.

And as we engaged gears we smiled
and waved. So we passed each other
but had shared the moment, witnessed it
clear as morning light and close.
I smiled for miles. I loved his face.

The New Allotment

It's here on the plan, she says: a grid
laid out pre-war, hers numbered 223.
Down from the taps, between high hedges,
past pyramids of beans, tomato vines,
maize, compost humming in a daze of wasps,
she counts the doors: parlour doors, shed doors,
front doors, one with a cat-flap, Shangri La,
Beware of the Dog, Eden, then the dog tied up
and docile. She sings along to a somewhere radio,
dum-de-dum-the-archers. It's 222, then 224,
and in between a hawthorn's overgrown her door.

Undeterred, jacket pulled up round her head,
she shoulders through and disappears,
reports back, *brambles, bindweed, dock leaves,
nettles,* her voice more distant, *there's a shed,*
she's shouting now, *roof good, chimney,
donkey-stove.* I can hardly hear her.
I'm sitting in the sun eating blackberries.
The radio's a wireless, *music-while-you-work,*
it's dig-for-victory times. I'm spitting seeds
and waiting by the fireweed.
She could be years in there.

The Bats

The summer after you had gone was hot,
the nights airless, every window open wide.
What woke me in the early hours, my book
fallen shut in my lap, wine-glass tipped,
was the ear-throb like a racing heart.
I thought it was a moth, and startled up
then saw the bat, a pipistrelle, circling
like a particle of night. I helped it find its way,
switched out the lights, opened two doors
to the starless dark, felt it pass my face.

The other bat I keep. It's in my freezer
laid out in tissue in a plastic box.
I found it on my doorstep, like a gift
wrapped in its wings, no sign of life.
Its open eyes are beads of jet, its teeth
white needle tips, its feet are hands,
its wings, spread out against the light,
an x-ray of fine bones, each thumb a hook.
I take it out from time to time to look
and stroke it, feel it soften, put it back.

Awake at 3.00am

This is the dead hour between
not yesterday, not yet tomorrow,
in which wakefulness is a gift, when
the house is unaware, as is the road
and going nowhere. The trees move close.

Be in this hour, the haunt of foxes
and owls – the cool dark of the room
at my back, my breath-cloud on glass.

The wind stirs the trees
as though it loves the air they breathe.
There is a light over the valley
where someone, in this given hour
listens to the trees, the owls.

Photograph: July 1951

How a day comes different, for being dressed
in a long pink frock which is just too long
so she will have to hold the hem and hop the puddles
on a path that stops at the church

where Jimmy Magee smokes a Woodbine
and talks so she can watch his words sputter,
stare, because she is too small to be minded.

By the way the mothers tip their heads together,
move their lips, something is being wrong,
by the way Jimmy's smoke is outbursts
and he grinds his foot on the church doorstep

where here come the flowers and the bride
under a cloud of net and smiling at the mothers
who are leaning back and smiling tight.

*

This is afterwards: me in the garden
by the gladioli which I'm nearly as tall as.
I'll want to keep the frock on.
It feels like a story on my legs.

Inventory: 15 The Green
(now William Hill's betting shop)

A worn way through from front to back,
the door that's open to the scullery and stairs,
a leather chair beside the empty grate,
the other of its pair, a window to the lane,
a view across to chapel, school and manse
and in the middle of the room, the table
with a drawer each end, one of them real –
the table that Aunt Peg will claim and sell,

the harmonium, its fretwork in the wood
with bellow-pedals that my feet don't reach
and all the yellowed keys that rattle
and the china stops, flute, oboe, clarinet,
I pulled to change the sound I couldn't hear –
the lost harmonium that bellows on dead air.

The Gift

My father chalked a line across the yard.
Walk this, he said. I did – then showing off
I turned a cart-wheel straight along it.
Next it was a rope, strung tight four feet
above the rows of cabbages and sprouts,
me, in my bare feet, sliding my easy weight.
On washing day I'd step between the pegs,
Mother warning me to *mind the whites*.

Don't look down, he said, and passed
the yard broom up to balance by.
When he confessed he'd never learned the art,
had fallen off the chalk, I took another step
and leapt into the garden's only tree,
up to the roof, over the town, free.

Sousa

it was babysitting for the vicar
that I saw a Buddhist monk self-immolate

I'd just come back from the kitchen
where I'd found an open bottle of communion wine
and the news was on
                              black and white
it was beautiful
his arms lifted on the grey flames
                                        eyes closed
rocking back and forwards like a meditation

when I told him what I'd seen
the vicar was disturbed
and insisted on playing Sousa marches
loud on his gramophone to help me over it

                    I won't forget
how a burning man looks before he drops

Drawing Water

The Art room was up its own staircase
over metal and woodwork, at the sea-end
of the oak-panelled school, kept apart
for the *hewers of wood and drawers of water*
of whom the headmaster spoke,
and who'd never do Latin or Greek.

But there Chalky White taught us to draw
what we see – the light on the windowsill plants,
how roof slates reflect the rhythm of chimneys,
that the sea spits light and swallows it, and colour
is split light, the ambiguous blue of the uplit fret,
grey-green like the moan and low of the foghorn,
calm as a mother's heart to her unborn,
blissful, like waves breaking, repeating.

High Wire Walk
Philippe Petit, 1974

A perfect dawn and I'm out on the wire,
feel its tensile weight, my rise and fall
with each tower's shift and sigh, up
with the gods in the air, the gods
in my feet, in every measured step.

If you can walk a straight line on the ground
you can walk a wire, ten feet, ten hundred feet,
no harness, net, trust counterpoise, learn
balance with the long pole, and you become
the pivot, your weight in your own hands.

They ask what runs through your mind;
it's the grace of the line, antiphony of breath,
the slow dance to an aeolian song. I was aware
of oil-burn on the thermals, the pall of city fumes,
the vapour trails dissolving into blue.

Time seems to hang up there. The wire
vibrates; think of the towers as cocoa tins,
a Babel-strum of voices rising through me,
messages trembling through my fingers
out along the pole into the sky.

I crossed eight times and, half way, rested,
stretched out full-length on my hammock-wire;
it lets the blood back to the toes, but you do it
for the cameras, for the crowd. They want,
they do not want, to see you falter, see you fly.

I had my comments ready for the press; tradition,
those showmen fired from cannons, dropped
in barrels over falls, my years of planning
as the towers rose, the training to be here,
the beating heart of the commercial world.

One step to go, one hundred thousand people
cheering, hanging out of windows, shredded paper
billowing around me. All I wanted was my feet
on solid ground, to live to tell my children,
my grandchildren, how I walked across the sky.

Driving Home from Grasmere
for Roy

There are in our existence spots of time
Which with distinct pre-eminence retain
A renovating Virtue, whence our minds
Are nourished and invisibly repaired.
     – The Prelude XI

You'd kept a thread of story spinning
down the M6 and through Cheshire,
over Macclesfield, past the Cat and Fiddle,
then we'd cut onto the track across Axe Edge.
You pointed – there the Dane gathers its water,
here, spoil heaps where Buxton men scraped coal –
poor stuff, enough to boil a kettle, warm a hearth.

It might have been at Thirkelow Rocks
or maybe the cairn on High Edge, but
we rounded the bend and stark on the crest
three horses were massive against the sky.
Something burned deep in the mind,
both of us, silent and clasping hands.

Did we slow then to see them lessen
down a shifting perspective, or tame them
with a story – the woman who said, *see those trees,*
when there's rain on the way they come near –
but I let go your hand and we carried on home.
A clear sky, the moon, at its perigee that night,
rolled full and close on our horizons.

He talks about fishing the Derwent,

not so much the catch and keep of it
but his preoccupation with the river,
knowing the urge of the course, his easy
stride through the chatter of thin water,
place of the dippers, or up to his waist
in deep hushes where mergansers dive,
home stretch of grayling and trout.

He makes flies from badger hair, feather,
mimics the damsel, caddis, the mayfly.
He speaks of the cast as a dance, the balance
of steady breath, the wish of the line reeling
out to the drop, knows the bite is a pleasure
not to be snatched, but a gentle bringing-in
like a good dog leashed, his hand, like sex
slipped under the fish's belly, held still
as the hook's sleeked out, so it hardly knows
as it glides away, that it was ever caught.

It's not just the fishing, he says,
but he's out of himself and part of the river.
He tells me his other story. It's dusk,
he's up near Shatton where the river cuts sharp
through shale, his feet numb with cold
and he's almost done, then he sees, he thinks,
a fresh-water mussel, but it's heavy in his palm.
Like this, he says, and pulls from his pocket
a Stone-Age axe-head, drops it in my hand.
Now this, he says, *is poetry.*

Identifying Scars

Wrist

up three floors to the flat and running
two steps at a time with the bottle of milk
(what was I thinking) keen to get back
tidy the place   put music on   soften the lights
I'm singing   scat-jazzing the stairwell

when my toe stubs the steel edge of a riser
and I'm falling into the explode of glass
the milk in a slow leap and cascade
over the lips of the steps   blue-white
veined with red and more and more red

Belly

run your finger down the furrow
the pucker and ruck like a misfitted zip
the six dimply nipples like a farrowing pig
from deep muscle sutures
the clamp and gash of fourteen metal clips
done by a man who couldn't stitch
     never again
     then again
but calm and expected   I watched them
reflected in the theatre's light fitting
up to their wrists in me
lifting her out like a rabbit

Finger

no wedding ring   though gold
might have saved the nerve
when again (years on)
I tripped on a tread
the bottle of claret
the tray of glasses
sprawled and shattered
the hand that saved me
stabbed on a sliver
that instantly deadened the finger

Head

two stitches I don't remember
except as the story of blood
and your panic   how I ran out
to the road and fell
when you screamed my name

towards the end   my brother and I
sit by your bed   when you wake
you say it will be okay
as long as you can see the bairns
across the busy road to school

Men who are lovers

will be on their toes, and if they say *love*
it's quickly, with no personal pronoun.
They'll prefer spontaneity, won't plan,
there'll always be a forgotten entry
in the already busy diary, a meeting,
family emergency, a missed last train.

They mean well, and whenever they can
will love to be in your home, your arms.
And when they've left on the early train
the house will echo with wine glasses
and Mahler's tenth. You will keep
an open heart, the outside light switched on.

Venice, October

Macroglossum Stellatarum

It's warm enough to eat on the terrace,
the old brick, still lizard-warm.
Look, she says, is that a hummingbird?
I know it's not: too small, no arc of beak,
but tongue uncurled and piercing

the geranium flowers. I've never seen
this moth but know it is a moth,
the fan-tail mimicry, perfected trick
of weightlessness. And it is day,
no candle burns. She needs me

to be sure. I am. Who she desires
is gone. I on the other hand, a stand-in,
know a moth when I see one, that no degree
of needing it to be a bird can make it so.
I hover in my own disturbance of the air.

Day Breaking

The first car of the day revs up the hill
and light comes stealthily and iron grey
because I spent the night hard in my heart,
and need another hour's grace to sleep.
So turn myself into the empty space,
to where you should have slept, and crave
your body's heat and musk, but meet
only the cold of unslept sheets. This day
without you breaks across my face.

Blue

Go through the gate by the railway line
and into the woods. Take the dog.
The rain has cleared the air, prepare
to breathe deep. The ants are humming,
you'll barely notice if they bite.
Brambles stray across the path.
Watch your step. The birds
sing clean as whistles, a song
like Bombay gin. Stop. Breathe it in.
Look uphill to the thick of the wood.
The light's switched on. Like neon.
This is the truth of blue. Whatever
you were thinking of is being forgotten.
Stay where you are. Each bell
gives up its blue to the mass, concentrates
on violet. The dog is very brown in blue.
Forget the sea, it has nothing to do
with this. All inland blue is gathered here.
If you walked thinking of sad blue eyes,
take this antidotal blue, its keen scent.
Do this every day, until blue
becomes white stitchwort, then green.
It will get hotter. Find another colour.

Familiar

it was the gestures of those hands
(such useful hands, and eloquent)
                reminded me
of when I watched
her hands undo a knotted rope
and felt the loosening
                and now I come to think
there was her throat, the tendons
of her neck tied to the carved wings
of her clavicles
                and might I mention
that the sharp articulation
of her speech through her decisive teeth
can hold me spellbound still.

which brings me to her lips.

but then I love my wide bed
to myself, the calm, clean white of it,
and I am truly over this.

Petrifying Well

The air here's full of spray and limey mist
that saturates the fiddleheads of bracken,
settles on a nest to turn three eggs to stone.

And that umbrella used to keep the rain
from long-dead heads until the rain was stone;
a boot, filled to its tongue, the laces furred

to threads of stone, so if you chiselled
layers back you'd find a foot of stone.
A baby's shoe remembers its first step;

a hat, its head; a teething ring, a spoon,
a sharp blade, blunted now, all stone.
Be still, in time see how it's done.

A six-inch iron key is locked in stone.
The baby is a man: the hat, the head
it fitted, emptied to its shell of bone.

Watch how the flux and sift dissolves
and then solidifies, ash to ash, dust
to stone. Stay, feel your neck grow stiff,

see droplets break in coronets of lime,
lose sense of time until your shoulders fix
and then, the petrifying of your spine.

At the Dental Technician's

I'm here for Aunt Danby's teeth.
He traces a finger along the row of grins,
the rank of gold-wired scrabble-tile blanks,
the cheery bubble-gum pink of gums.
And I know which is hers, recognise
the enamelled front of her smile
even without the puckered up kiss
of her lipsticked lips. I point.

He shows me the mend, the rivet,
the seal, and I marvel how narrow
how tight the horse-shoe curve,
the nibbley bite she does, pincer sharp,
how white, how bleak the ivories
she'll whistle through, tunelessly.

Sleepless and Sixty

There was a party, champagne, gifts,
one when I opened it, confettied silver sixties,
a star-burst celebration over the lanterned yard.
When everyone had gone I couldn't sleep,
each crease in the sheet a knife-edge, pillows
were rock, quilt, the weight of the world.
As the kettle whistled on the stove, a full moon
glittered like a bad joke on the yard.

On the second day of my seventh decade,
coffee outside, and the sun shone on a lace
of snail trails, a mass moluscal glean of crumbs,
and each had visited a sixty, and finding it inedible,
moved on. I swept them up, threaded a necklace
on silk through every zero, threw it away.

The Best Thing

The best thing in the world
is to make the house ready, check each room
for temperature, smooth the sheets, plump pillows,
look through every window to enjoy the various views.
The houseplants will be spruced, flowers
freshly cut and casually arranged.

The stove is warm, the smell in the sunlit kitchen
might be coffee, or rising bread, or toast
(the best smell in the home is toast) or hyacinths,
which today are a promise of Spring.
The house this Spring day is ready, every room of it.
The house is ready. Where is everybody.

from *From Matlock to Mamelodi (2011)*

Lucid Dreaming

It's when I drift back into early morning sleep
I travel most. This morning it was Margaret Lax
I visited, and she was as she was, Bardot,
blonde hair falling round her face, pouting lips.
I'd called to see her at her mam's in Hartlepool
and her gran was still in bed in the alcove,
her leg propped against the fireplace,
NHS wig on the chair. It wasn't fair to laugh.
We went down to the Fish Sands where
it was Summer, hot seaweed popping, fishermen
on The Heugh. It was time for honesty,
remembering the wet kelp in the face that night
on Arran, but when I turned to speak, she'd gone.

String Quartet

First Violin: this instrument will take him by surprise,
                  from time to time will lift him off his feet.

Second Violin: watchful and relied on, both man and violin,
                  see how the heart will almost close his eyes.

Viola: what passions of the mind and body: the grace
                  and accents that will move his feet to dance.

Cello: she and her instrument, the composition triangular
                  as Raphael, the sound, blood deep, lit like an angel.

Alone in the hall she limbers her fingers,
is warming her cello, easing the strings.
A slow chromatic scale climbs note by tone
and sinks back down, is pelvic, femoral.
Faster then and sure, each new note
gathers up those freed onto the air,
arcs of bowed chords filling this vast space.

He's ready, patient, leans against the stage,
his violin held easy on his collar bone.
He bends to it like a fiddle-player in a bar,
head tipped as though listening to a secret.

Rehearsal:

Into a gathered silence which is the true beginning,
an attention in the brow, the lift of shoulder, one breath drawn,
the first chord, nerved on the lips, the tongue, a kiss.

And now her cello's cradling their song, and they reply,
to lift her so her bone-deep sound will pour
into the moments when a silk sheet, like a billowing cloud,
begins to settle round.
                    Again and then again, until it's time to begin.

Gershwin: Lullaby
Lavista: Reflejos de la Noche

The evening's warm: cicadas underscore
the fading light, the scent of rosemary
and moonflowers: the children sleep.

So take me in your arms, my face
resting on the muscle of your shoulder,
and what we feel is where this rhythm is,

the belly and the hips, the sway we pivot on –
navel, pubic bone – a tango slowed
to almost sleep, beneath the hot moon.

Ravel: String Quartet in F

This was on the radio today,
an old recording, and I listened
through a haze of crackles, hiss of time.
And years from now if you remember me,
might it be like that, something wordless,
nerved on the skin, the lips, the tongue.

Chevening

Fine cotton thread, sky-blue, eight strands,
the needle eye just big enough to pull it through,
and long: you don't want knots, loose ends
to rub against the skin. These stockings,
pale flesh-pink, fit smooth and snug.
Thirty pairs to finish while there's light to count
the stitches, rows, and keep the tension right.

On Sunday it's the Harvest Feast. The bosses
will fork out. There'll be a band and pies and all,
and ladies with their lace and disapproving lips
all looking down their high and mighty noses
at us pretty girls, us *flirts* – skilled seamers
who have turned their heels, whose chevening's
embroidered up their shins. We know how tight
their garters are, we know what's up their skirts.

It's girls like us should know our place, be grateful.
Me, I'd like to run, get on a ship, work my passage
to a better world. But for today, twenty pairs to go.

Luminary

Set the scene with a full bright moon,
note Flamsteed's Crater in the Ocean of Storms,
the impact; now think of the tide-swell,
the collision and ferment of curious minds,
a beginning, then, of modern times.

So at full-moon they come to Erasmus,
unfolding ideas like charts, maps to a future,
these friends – the maker of buckles, the potter,
the clock-maker working with minutes,
but dreaming of eons, engineers, mechanics,

and you, Joseph Wright, artist and witness,
frame new perspectives, cast your light
on these moments advancing the times.
We think of you stretching your canvas, mixing
a spectrum of colour, planning balance and form.

Those intimate nocturnes – faces, keen and alight,
drawn close by the candle's flame; and there,
a lamp is the sun, and the orbit of planets, moon,
demonstrates an eclipse; in the foreground,
another – the dark silhouette of a child.

There, is the clamour and heat of the air
in the blacksmith's forge, a glimpse of moon
behind clouds; and the same moon shines
as the Alchemist kneels, like prayer, and gasps
at the instant, the phosphorous flare.

You write from Italy, wishing John were there
to see Vesuvius redden the sky, say
that he would think deeply into the mountain
while you skim the surface, the glare in darkness,
the moon floating palely over the bay.

John is our clock-maker. He explains the heave
and uprising that opened up strata, like pages
recording the layers of time. You paint him,
pen and diagram in his hands, a smoking volcano,
the image you choose for the power of his mind.

You give us your views in the changing light,
Arkwright's Mill, Matlock Tor, Dovedale
by day, by night, and the stories you frame
come like news from your time. You set these scenes,
the storm and the vision of these luminous minds.

The Dome and the Foucault Pendulum
Buxton, February 26, 2008

We watch the traced ellipses of its swing
that prove the solid ground we stand on
moves through day to night and back again.

The Dome's vast air's a sounding drum
that listens as I speak, and plays my words
back half a second late – the interruption
shocks, my ghost voice spins me round,
unnerved to find myself beside myself.

That night the earth's skin shudders
underneath my house. Torn from a dream,
I think my heart's arrhythmia's the cause –
the sound of clattering windows, moan
in the piano strings – then wide awake, discover
pictures fallen from the walls, a ceiling cracked,
plaster flakes, glass fish on the bathroom floor.

Next day in the Dome the talk is earthquake.
The electromagnetic pulse kicks in to prove
the pendulum's point. I speak behind my back;
my footsteps follow as I leave.

Collecting Entries for the Bestiary

Eyam

The morning after I had held the gold
of fox eyes in my torch beam, I find
the scattering of feathers, the snapped
bill of the white drake's mate.
A cold day. Above the top field
the kestrel cruises the wind,
balances on a knife-point.

Arbor Low

Here is a dish to catch the north light,
a bowl to gather distance, which
echoes with the liquid call of curlews,
broadcasts lapwings, lark song.
Stones whiten as the day fades,
night settles in the wake of a car
racing Long Rake from Parsley Hay.
Lights start up like beacons, cairn to tor.
Feel what this place is for.

Upper Padley

I know nothing of horses in July
so walking the track by the Dutch barn
it was a hulk of shadow stopped me
and its quiet breath. The dark gathered
around a doze of flies, became horse,
and a grey fly-mask drawn down

from its exact ears to its nose.
I thought it hooded to be stilled
in its own dark, and waiting
to be taken into another.
I was afraid for it
and did not speak.

Chatsworth: Bees in the Lime Tree

We have danced our lines from hive
to blossom, heavy legged with pollen.

Under the canopy's gloss of heart-leaves,
the flowers' froth, the scent is honey sweet.

Rest here from the high sun, where we,
pendant as clustered fruits, have stilled

our wings, lost in the anaesthesia of lime,
and one by one we will forget our flight,

trust air to catch us as we drop
into your hair, your lap.

Cressbrook

... a gentleman to whom it was allotted on an inclosure,
has made a plantation of lavender, peppermint, and
other aromatic herbs, and set up a distillery ....
— William Bray 1778

Before the mill, before the village and the name
John Taylor's house leant into Rubicon Wall,
shade-cool and calm by Water-cum-Jolly.
All under water now, lost beneath the mill-pool
on the Wye, the rows of peppermint and lavender,
the beds of cress in Grass Brook.

Go now to the stretch of pretty water,
the enclosure of the cliffs. A heron
lifts its weight muscling the bulk of air,
swans turn water to glass.

The dale holds its breath, a whisper
on the waterskin, so as you walk
you enter something like a holy place
where water is the host, its molecules
remembering sweet calming herbs, the cure
of swansdown for the heavy heart.

Properties of Water

Some mornings the valley's drowned
under a white sea, so calm and dense
you could row across to Mother Cap,
look out from Higger Tor, set sail
for the archipelago of Win Hill, Lose Hill,
cross the Great Ridge to Mam Tor.

But it's only the Derwent sleeping, only
the breath of its dreams, remembering
ice and melt, the shouldering
of stone, the shift beneath the shales.
And the sun sees through, lights
heathers, cotton grass, and gorse,
so the river wakes, stretches,
to find itself as usual, on course.

Ferreting

'You'll never see a predatory animal that's ugly'
– Simon Whitehead, Pakefield Ferrets

It is their nature to be fleet,
eyes aglint in sweet sleek faces,
pink-lipped and tongued, razor teeth.
At play in the run, a roil of fur,
a fesnyng knot of ferrets unravelling.
They chew on chicken bones, and stink.

It is their business to be fleet
and sleek in warrens, to ferret out
the rabbits into nets, or to the jaws of dogs.
It's quick, humane and green, all good –
the crops are saved, the rabbit meat
is *tweedy-cordon-bleu*. I am convinced.

I want to hold a ferret.
I want to eat a rabbit.
I check his web-site – YouTube,
where he necks a rabbit
to the tune of Samuel Barber's
Adagio for Strings.

Companion Stone

In the 18th Century, guide stoops were placed to help travellers across treacherous Derbyshire moorland. Typically square in section, and standing up to five feet tall, they indicate directions to local market towns.

Each companion stone has been placed near an original stoop, each one designed by an artist, and inscribed with a poem, directing not to a town, but to the future.

Ann worked with artist Kate Genever, and poet Jo Bell. They collaborated to make two stones which relate to each other and are placed in Longshaw Park.

walk on
by water-flow
by crow-flight
by night by
star by
satellite
by map by
stone
& so to
home

On the underside of the stone (to be discovered maybe in a few hundred years) is the following inscription, inspired by Ken Wilson, local farmer, who has re-cycled many millstones, in walls, and as his farmhouse doorstep.

re-use
this stone
for wall
for stoop
or
step
as a
threshold

walk on
by water-flow
by crow-flight
by night by
star by
satellite
by map by
stone
& so fo
hom

Shot Put

Three hours a day, six days a week for years
and years, priming the power in my muscles,
steeling the springs of my mind, for this
and now – the familiar weight cupped in my hand,
the cold curve on the pulse in my neck.
Turn my back to the field, turn into my heart,
find balance, then all of my gathered strength
flows into the dance, hop and swoop, perfect turn
and the fire forges through me into the thrust,
all the hours and weeks and years of it, launching,
propelling four kilos of steel up, far and away.

Later Uncollected Poems (2006 – 2012)

Anatomical

Run a finger down from throat to sternum,
find the catch, and spring the casements wide,

undo the zip down to the pubic bone,
turn back the flesh like opening a winter coat.

It's dark inside, where kidneys, liver,
wallow deep red in their juices.

A sigh of unaccustomed air picks colours out,
surprising yellows, granular, an olive tone

behind the pancreas which cannot say precisely
what it's busy at. The diaphragm

can't help itself, its sink and rise,
but tremulous this morning, shallow.

What was I looking for? A blade, a stone,
a reservoir or well, something out of true

or misaligned? I see there's room for a heart
that's regular, though tight with the weight of mine.

But it was good to air this, look closely in,
now shut myself up, fasten, zip, replace my skin.

False-Widow Spider

The sun-shade was cobwebbed
from its winter in the shed,

and up there where the spokes met,
was a gleam of jet,

an abdomen round as a bean,
its thorax a bead

and all eight legs, articulated steel.
And stretching them out of its sleep

it saw two dozen of me, gazing
up out of forty-eight brown eyes

so it dropped like a stone
on its belay thread

onto one of my heads.
We were all surprised by the scream.

Last Notes

Four pianos on Cromer prom, unwanted,
seen better days. I find one still in tune,

strike a chord, run scales, and play
a few remembered bars of Claire de Lune.

Officials put the barriers up,
the teams begin, the aim –

dismantle a piano, post the pieces
through a foot-square slot, the fastest wins.

Wire-cutters to the strings, each twang a dull tone
as the tension snaps. Sledge-hammer at the case

until its jaw sags and the teeth fall out.
The soundboard's axed, the hollowness exposed,

its nerves unstrung, stripped to a skeleton frame,
dull gold, its breaking hard and loud.

And the whole thing drops to its knees,
wire, old iron, firewood, ivory keys.

The Book (Being Dead – Jim Crace)

All endings should be unresolved, untidy,
things will remain undone despite the time
spent organising drawers and filing documents
and burning the evidence of shame on garden fires.
The preparations that you make are wasting energy
and time. Look how your carriage clock is ticking still
it feeds on time. This book is hardback, cerulean blue,
the endpapers funereal, the lettering on the spine is gold
and if he makes death's narrative a poem
    the signals of distress it sent, were stars
do not believe him. All endings must be unresolved,
your store, so neatly filed, of passions,
and all memory, gone.
Do not make plans to go – make plans to carry on.

Exits

1.

M6/M61: Here is a no-man's land,
a wild park islanded by slip-roads,
by the constant go of carriageways.
Somehow he ended up there, pitched
his one-man tent in the last place
anyone would think to look for him.
How long before the rushed hours dulled
to dark noise, closed in to insect-drone,
the kestrel's hover-search and drop.
Nights were strobed by lights,
carbon gases, oil-burn, fumed
like incense on his dislocated breath.
When did he zip his tent shut, lie down
in the last place he would be found.

2.

M1: It was late and there were miles to go,
but traffic was light. He might have yawned,
shuffled, stretched, tuned in to Easy Listening
on Classic FM, felt the road rush under him
until the world was in reverse and he seemed still.
Maybe the music faded to the wheels' thrum,
his grip relaxed and his foot went slack.
Cameras clocked him at ninety, saw him drift,
caught in the slip-stream of a convoy of HGVs,
veer back, slow down, coast to a stop.
He woke, dry-lipped, to blue lights flashing,
a policeman gripping his arm, juggernauts passing.
He says he will not drive that stretch again,
certain he'll meet his own ghost waiting.

3.

M42: After leaving you it takes three hours
to get back home, and on the last long run,
the sun is sinking to my left, and mist rises
from the open fields. I imagine the cool of it
swathed around my legs, striding through,
the car on the hard shoulder, engine running.
The day is running to ground, its gold
sifting through the trees. The motorway
becomes a murmur I will not notice, the mist,
a veil snagged on hawthorns heavy with blossom,
where I am still: the only sound is a leaf stirring;
all I feel is the breeze on my face,
then not that, the sense of my breath,
the heart's pulse, not even that.

The Self

The sentence begins with
lock and key, miscarriage
of logic, lost in the mists,
but on high-day-holidays,
wine and sun, an amnesty.
But it bolted, ran off with a dream,
lost years, travelling, moving on.

Then, unexpectedly, home in the night,
switching on lights, rattling
through drawers for the cheese-knife,
cork-screw, and the stories it told,
curled up by my side, smelling
of salt and patchouli and fags.

There were times when it crept up
and pushed from behind, *can-do*,
that turned into *who do you think
you must be*, then snatched
at my feet from under the table, my bed,
tied my laces together, tight.

These days I see its disguise,
chameleon, pipistrelle-in-the-freezer,
sit it down at my table, insist
it washes the dishes, stays true, comes clean.

Aerial Views

1. Victoria Falls – tourist map 1970

Not legends, but details drawn
as though from photos taken from a plane –
rain forest and shrub, red earth tracks
to *Curio Sellers, Field Museum,*
and *Customs*, a black line ruled
at the border with Rhodesia.
And the stretch and glint of blue,
the urge and rush at *Danger Point, Boiling Pot*,
white-water rage at *Knife-Edge Bridge*.

I have a photo of you there –
plastic mac, a rainbow at your shoulder.
I can almost hear the constant roar.

2. BBC 'Coast', 2002

They're doing Yorkshire:
the helicopter's traced the coast line from the Tees
and hovers over Whitby. There's the Abbey,
the hundred and ninety-nine steps to Church Street.
Look, people are waving. There's Gossips' Yard,
the house you'd rented for your honeymoon,
the view across the estuary to the fish quay.
The gulls are wheeling, the tide high.

3. Google Earth – Satellite, 150 ft

Like flying from my desk:
bank south-west over sea, cross Europe,
how many screens to Africa, how long
to pan the globe and back again.

I'm up above your house.
They've built on at the back,
knocked the shed down, parked their car
where you planted roses at the side.

I want to tell you
but you're nowhere to be found,
not if I searched each inch of Earth,
no trace of you, not anyplace.

My Passionate Father

He rang the bell to stop the bus
and from the platform
yelled across the High Street,
                    Rya, Rya.
It was market day.
Everything stopped.
Everyone looked this way.
We shrank in our seats.
                    Rya, Rya.
And like a spotlight picked her out
she turned and walked towards us
through the parting crowd.

We were silent as the bus moved on,
our mother's cheeks flaming, her lips tight.

Billingham Central Library

Before I learned to read
this was the mystery of books.

We would enter the church of them,
our feet on the polished floor

and I would sit on the lowest shelf
while she ran her hand's salute

along high rows, until she found the book
a good book, and bowed her head, her lips

murmuring her prayer. This was the place
where all quiet lived, where in my patience

I absorbed the scent of print, whispers
of the turned page, and the ritual at the altar,

a dedication stamped like affirmation
into the gift of every chosen book.

Distaff Line

Don't believe this yet, but when
you have closed my dark eyes,
spread flowers round my face,
and roses in my cold hands, it will be
in the night you feel arms like a lover's
and sigh and stir, but it will be me.
By morning you will wear my skin.

The mirror will alter the look of your eyes,
when you comb your hair, feel my skull,
hear my voice say something that means
that's nice, my good girl. The song
you sing will be breath lost for words,
and your dance, heavy, with me
on your feet, the ache of my weight
spun into your heart for three long years.

When the last year brittles my skin
to a husk, keep the shreds, the wisps
of hair, roll them tight into a ball
then catch the loose thread and spin.
You will unravel me stitch by loop and seam,
my hands held out to you for the winding in.

Brick

We all agreed he was,
good sort, do anything
for anybody, open doors
and hold them wide,
fresh breath of air,
a breeze, for granted,
true, a stop-gap, paper-weight,
until he dropped it, toe-stub
tripped, shouted out
a ton-fall on our heads.
Whatever next.
We strung a line, layer
mortared over layer,
tidy, straightened out,
and high, to block the view.

Padley Woods: June 2007

How the trees love this weather:
slaked hydraulics pulse on full power,
their trunks, drenched conduits as they lean
into the long moment of their fall.

Water streams the paths, finds new ways
down and lays washed sand in its wake.
Tree roots, spreading like knuckled veins
over the slopes, are terraces of sand and silt.

The music of the gorge is white water,
its constant industry of flow, the brook
full of itself and urgent for the river,
shifting wood, moving rock, carving stone.

At the bridge the water's hurl is leather brown
and heady – on the road, springs erupt and well
through tarmac, streams find their way easy
through dry-stone walls. The canopy is listening

its tesserae of leaves held out palm-up
and tapping a morse of *rain, more rain* – then louder,
loud as the brook's full throated song, clattering –
rain, here it is, again and more of it, rain more rain.

The Ashop Dreams under Ladybower

Once in my own time I gathered moss,
steeped bracken's dying ochre reds,
churled a course into the cleft of hills,
adjusted to each drought and freeze,
ran full and fast, and always found my way.
I knew well how to smooth a rock, or finger
through a fallen sheep to find the bones,
but then this wall rose up and stoppered me.
Backwashed, stretched, I forced
an entry into gardens, lapped at doors,
sank and probed through empty graves
then up the aisle into the apse, and day
by week climbed higher up the tower.
Now I am full to my brim,
describe the valley whole,
turn the hillside on its head,
have time to take the colours of the sky.
But I still run deep and my back,
my shoulder's to that wall.

The Singing and Dancing

For Lucas

He calls them the Spookinesses,
can't remember all of their names
as they look all alike in blue dresses,
dark eyes, long yellow hair
to their waists, and they're playing
with him, hide and seek.

The reason for time, he says,
is without it, everything happens at once
and he can't find Spookiness thirteen.
The others line up with their hair
and clean hands, but their faces
are dirty and covered in soot.

He sings them all home – Angela, Beryl,
Caroline, Dora – his timing is perfect
so Zoe comes down from the chimney
and they're all of them dancing
yellow hair flying, footprints
all over the carpet.

Touching a Jackson Pollock
The Metropolitan Museum of Art: 2009

In New York they let you get real close
to the paintings. You can near enough
smell the resins, like the oil's still wet,
and the man with paint on his boots
has just stepped away, wiping his hands.

My brother hangs back, needs a break,
his inhaler, a drink.
                    In the museum cafe,
where just beyond the plate glass wall
a vagrant in the park strips to his shorts,
pours water over his head and chest,
                    I chatter about his painting –
how he'd have his canvas hard down
on the ground, come at it from all sides,
the dance of it, repeated steps, the arc
and sweep, fractals of splatters and trails,
that out of chaos, patterns emerged.

My brother orders another drink.
Outside a cop deals with the naked man.

Back in the gallery, we're looking close,
so near the guard warns, *step back ma'am*.
Set in the layers of flung paint, a bottle top,
cigarette butt, broken glass. The guard
turns away. My brother reaches out.

Mother's Egg Slicer

I don't believe she ever used it.
I did, loved the guillotine precision
of eight wires through hard-boiled egg,
perfect discs spaced on buttered bread,
but more, the way each wire
plucked a different note, a scale
nobody had heard before, strummed
arpeggios that tuned the ear far away,
to blue silk kimonos like the one
my uncle brought back from the east,
the hobbled steps of tiny feet, the flirt
of painted fans, or the eggshell china
light shone through, a dragon's egg,
a dance of something yet unhatched.

Dancing to La Creation du Monde, *Darius Milhaud*

He put the record on and said
what can you do. The room became
the world and its dancing floor.

And the world was my arms,
a beach ball space my heart wrapped itself around.
I was strong as a silverback, around me
a forest roamed with sprung water and parakeets.

In all this I was light
as mid-day, a high sun
electric in each bone.

Duet

(En Bateau – Debussy*)*

somewhere else
he plays the lower notes,
leans right across the keyboard
fingers fumbling at the missing melody.
the major key seems wrong, he can't sing

soprano, is out of his depth, and pedalling
for two, the echoes clash and jangle.
he should return against the flow
but fears deep water, undertow,
and is without an oar.

she has set her chair
to the right of middle C to play.
when the left hands should lead to the right,
she counts in her head, marks time with her foot,
carries on with the flow of triplets that ripple away.

she hears it all, is sailing along, her quiet hum
of the absent bass, not heard on the street
where a man stands still to listen
to a dance composed for a leg
and a child hops by.

Peter Grimes

fish sing red-gilled in his dreams

shoals and shoals
$\qquad$ swimming the sea's mobius flows

he sleep-talks
his voice
$\qquad$ a clarinet blowing the words
$\qquad$ to no absolute meaning

sirens and storm
$\qquad$ fists at the windows
a blood thirst
$\qquad$ lashed on the summon of horns
follow him
follow him
$\qquad$ down to the bay

the organ plays in the seamen's chapel
choristers gape like fish out of water
sing catches and nets in augmented chords

then bold
$\qquad$ a calm innuendo
sung out in unison
$\qquad$ clear and loud

day breaks as splinters of glass on the sea
his cry is the gulls weeping
sandpipers stabbing red shells on the shore
the sea's resolution lapping the blood away

The Hour

The early light was shrill with snow,
the road white-over, still untracked.
I'd got the date all wrong, the clocks
had not moved on but I believed they had.

You had a plane to catch.

A reckless drive, I'd hardly slept,
was maybe still a little drunk,
but we arrived intact, to find
the hour we'd lost was waiting
between check-in and *Boarding now
Gate Five*: a sober hour, our goodbye
seemed as long as Mahler's Ninth.

You rang from Le Pont des Arts.

But that was years ago, and still
each autumn, spring, as time adjusts,
that same hour's given, taken back,
and the Ninth draws out the loss.

The Composer's Hands

The pianist begins,
and the composer listens,
his hands clasped on his lap like prayer,
or more,
        as though they cupped a bird
that is learning a new way to sing.

His fingers tremble scales, pick out
with small insistences, each bar,
each stress.

        His eyes are closed,
his fingertips a seismograph of score.

The passage comes,
        a gathering crescendo
like bloodrush,
        so one hand flies up,
released, his fingers spread
as though on a draught of wings.

4.45pm, Winter

This is the time of day I'll die,
a time for running down, a lull.
The light has almost gone,
birds have uttered anxious cries
and homed, and on the radio,
no voices now, but evensong
to mark the pace into the night.
The kettle has sung, tea in a china cup
will cool while the body slackens
in its easy chair, feet up,
head cushioned, all its days' weight
given up to the darkening sky.
Allow this halting tea-time rest,
this regular rehearsal of death.

Return

for Sheila and Clitheroe John

and we took to the floor and flew, one two three
hop and turn, the room spinning round, our feet
barely skimming the ground, we were light
and air, nothing else but the dance, then and there,
the flight of it, perfect, propelling us faster
and lighter, carried along on a soaring force.

That was the night before
he was dropped through the sky
to land beneath billowed silk.
He never came back.

These days her hips are bad, her heart
not good, but sometimes she feels again,
the heat of a hand, the surge of that force,
filled with it, driving her on. Days like this,
she says, she's dancing the polka with John.

Learning the Sonatas

K.570

Mr O'Neil says, *practice this with all the repeats, it's like
a conversation, a statement and response.* She plays, and then
again, the second time it gathers up the echo of the first and is
most satisfied, each pattern, like a story's thought, turns back
to its first idea, then full of itself, slides and slots like jigsaw
to the next melodic line, and no repeat's repetitive, but a dance
that spirals in its mobius loop. And so it builds, an ornate tower
of sound she climbs into, a place to visit and then own.

Her father's stripped the wallpaper, the carpet's up, curtains down,
the room's an echo-box he whistles in, his cigarette smoke coiling
from the ashtray. She's in the Allegretto, fingers chasing loops
of scales, the melodies fly out through open windows to the street,
where neon lights snap on in cannon, to the slap of skipping ropes
and voices chanting *all-in-together-girls-one-and-two-and-three:*
her father dances Chaplin's heel-clicks round the room,
then slides the pasted paper matching patterns that repeat.

K.545

The most familiar sonata, the one that everybody knows
and even my mother whistles underneath her breath.
On the street an ice-cream van chimes the opening bars
just as the TV plays, in black and white, the brass notes
of the theme for Coronation Street.

We're on the sofa, each with a cone
of lime and vanilla ice, she smiles,
as she does when she watches TV.
The chimes play Mozart streets away.

These days, as I play the opening bars,
I taste vanilla and lime,
hear Coronation Street,
and see again her smile,
a full C major chord.

K.332

Once, during the adagio, she felt his shadow on the keys.
Not just her hands working the score, but her body
driven to its muscle, tight in the belly, in her thighs.

(her teacher said, when Mozart played,
his perfect sound was broadcast to the universe,
and that a true performance could tune
into his frequency and call him home.)

She has lost herself in this sonata. The room, the house,
the air is full of him, the progressions of his scales
and chords. As though her hands were not her own.

Fair Flora Wood

Not that we were looking for her
or knew who she was, why she was there.

But if I say the birds were hushed,
a breeze shivered in the brittle leaves
then stilled, and rose-bay willow herb
breathed out its down onto the air, you say
you don't remember when, or where.

But you held the dog lead tightly
when his hackles rose, you heard
the warning purr rise in his throat,

and we were silent at her feet, her looking down
as though she knew we'd come, and when
we reached to touch her hand she seemed
to move, and then the withered necklace
of spring flowers fell to the ground.

We never spoke of it till now.
You must remember how it was.

Calling the Owls
For Annabel

Between the moon and the rising tide
curlews pour their last notes on the sand,
bats tune the dulling light, the owl-call starts.

She is a shadow on the dark field
who tips her head to cast a call
from the hollow where her sternum
meets her collar-bones, the screech exact,
and so the owl replies, calls out to her bones,
and glides close to ruffle her hair, caught out
scoops back its voice like prey to roost.

Her bright tongue raised into the night
the scope of her throat, her light laugh
in the effort of it, breaking.

Sheltering

She was in a call box, soaked,
hair dripping, feet cold and wet,
waiting for the storm to pass.
Through the steamy panes
the tip and bob of umbrellas,
the guttering stream,
rain stotting off the road.
And then the telephone rang.
She let it ring until it stopped,
she couldn't be the right one,
in the right place.
The wind got up, the light
was fading, she had missed her bus,
would have another hour to wait.
And then the telephone rang,
louder than she could bear –
stale breath in the mouthpiece,
grease against her ear –
Is it you, are you there, he said,
and into her silence
someone was singing,
until she said, yes,
this is me, I'm here.

When it was said

the earth's tectonic plates slid suddenly apart
and in the wake a jug of milk trembled
on its tipping point, but not before a dozen eggs
were dropped, shells on the polished floor
and nowhere to tread carefully, and then
the heavens broke, the skies lashed out
and rained like it could never stop.
the window blew wide open off its latch
and fricatives of draught collapsed
a patient tower of cards, plosives
ripped the calendar page by page until
a year wished back, and then rushed on
to snow and ice, and lilies scattered stains
and petals on the open book of hours,
and dice rolled off the table, through the door.
the rain stormed, choked in gutters,
stammered off the roads until they streamed,
the brook rose, its heart so full it sprang
its wooden bridge and skewed it to the rocks.
caverns sang as water bellied in and forced
the faults and shafts, pit props caved, ground
dropped away from under someone's feet
and the house foundations groaned. a gritstone
boulder that had leaned a million years into its fall
fell and rolled over and over and over, down
to the river's waters stretched into the town
where furniture floated away, a TV set, a bed,
the table that bore the emphasis of fists,
all carried on the spate, with eggs and pottery
and tropes of cards and dice stacked up
against the odds of pages turning back again,
when at last it was said, it was all said and done.

From the Household Book of Spells

(chapter 1: smoke and mirrors)

i) for the invitation

At the window hold a mirror firm and horizontal,
catch a pool of light. A hawk will circle, hover.
Listen: the sway of trees, the birds' alarm,
then footsteps. Raise the glass at arms' length –
a ricochet of sun, a shadow moving at its frame,
behind you, the sofa by the blazing fire, beyond,
the hall, the stairs – now let the doorbell ring,
take time to gaze into your own dark eyes, enough
for your reflection to strike back, and further
back, smaller, smaller still, before you turn
and call, *come in,* again, *come in.*

ii) for stopping time

Try this: unplug electrical appliances
including mobile phones, turn clocks
face down, mirrors to the wall.
Together, read a John Donne poem,
reduce the whole world to one room.
Meet eyes, hands, lips, what comes
won't pass – fly trapped in amber,
light fractured in a crystal.
But be aware of danger,
don't wish too hard, eternity is final.

iii) for breakages

This day might come. Hawks kill,
winds change, the mirror lies
and cracks. In this eventuality,
discard, don't look into the splinters
of your eyes, your broken face,
try kindness, compromise.
Failing that, keepsake, token, effigy.
Do not resort to pins, slivers of glass.

iv) for which there is no spell

for creeping damp that freezes on the windowsill
for flies that gather on the glass and die
for the cellar cold as death and racked with bottles
for promises that come to nothing after all
for the empty acre of the bed you lie in
for nights not knowing how to close your eyes
for winter turning into spring with no more magic
there is no spell, no spell. abide.

v) for infestations

Ignore the skitterings of mice, mercurial
silverfish which are the husks of shadow,
hobthrush rolling crumbs under the rugs,
leave them be. For mites and fleas, no spell,
a tip: desert the house for seven days,
then send a black cat in to walk the emptiness.
The bugs latch on. Dispose of cat and them.
More difficult, the house possessed
of a shade, the way a smell, a taste,
a symphony, will bring it home.
Smoke it out. Skin cells, wisps of hair,
emails, CDs, gifts, Facebook wall,

ignite with cognac in a frying pan.
Admire the blue exploring flame. Carry it
from room to room, repeat, *enough, be gone.*
Don't get your fingers burned,
and do it only if the riddance is for good.

vi) for stubborn stains

Some stains respond to flannel and soft soap.
For bigger spills, soak up with soda, flour,
lavender-scented talc, and brush off
with a rabbit's scut. For residues, apply
opposites: lemons for oil, white wine for red,
tears for blood. If that's no good, pick
cotton grass at dawn still wet with dew,
withered lambs' tails snatched from the crow,
or simply spit. Some stains are deep,
like the dark spread on the marble hearth,
the glass of wine tipped in the sudden move
to take into your arms the sorry man
who warmed by your fire, and wept.
That dulled shine, acid biting into stone,
memento, shade, is permanent.

vii) for disappearing

Don't answer the phone.
Wait for days for no-one to call.
Don't sleep much. Try not eating.
Fade, until the fullest moon
shreds its light through hawthorn,
then go to the top of the garden.
Listen as the owl prepares to hunt,
voice soft as a pigeon. A decision:
make your bed among the nightshade

and valerian, or look across the dark lawn
to the kitchen, where your wraith
washes her hands under a running tap,
wrings out a cloth. Go back to her
before she locks the door
and switches off the light.

Killing Time in Tate Britain

It's more than twenty years since I was here,
and if it was the icy wind on Vauxhall Bridge unravelled me,
hair in my face, stinging my eyes, it is this marble space, the air
of preservation, assembles me. It's hours before we'll meet.

Those years ago, I bought a print, Rossetti's *Proserpine*, the sex
of her lips, her mass of hair: see now the imminence of loss.
(It hangs, framed still, on my grown-up daughter's wall.)

I'm in the Turner Rooms, drawn closer to his studies:
Figures in a Storm: Sunlight on Ruins: how his later vision's
tuned to momentary effects of light, refracted prisms of watery air.
Then I'm waiting, drinking coffee in the basement, making sense
of Francis Bacon's passionate disintegrations of the flesh.

Next day I'm on the train for home and writing it all down:
odd things: *man with twenty-two umbrellas in his arms: girl
on her knees sweeping litter from the street: the shimmer
of eucalyptus leaves in St James's Park – and how
the birds sang through the night like dawn outside our room,
the wind playing the flagpoles in a minor chord –*

and through the fast window, signs of an early spring
and sunlight catching on my ring, the ring my daughter loves.
It glitters on the marcasite, warms the pale cabechons of quartz.
I imagine it on her hand. Imagine her holding it to the light.

Disappearing Tricks

like this: blindfold, reaching out,
fingers feathering for touch. *warmer.*
turn to the voice. *no colder, cold.*
muffled laughter. then a silence.
face lost inside the knotted scarf,
damp around my mouth and nose,
stifling, so rip it off to find
the blinding light of an empty room.

and like this. those girls at school
who set me up with a blind date.
I waited hours. he didn't show.
next day, the letter from him via them,
explaining why, and saying
such things so I replied. then notes
of teenage love exchanged, until I saw
what passed between them. foxes. snakes.

it was like this when you lied.
it was like this when I learned
how long you'd lied. blindfold.
foxed. you, snake-charmed
up a rope you pulled up after you.

What's Left

just bone, and teeth – familiars
to a muscled tongue that's gone,
but spoke of the flight of birds over a house
where bats would roost under the roof,
the night sky with perpetual moths,
a sky-line that's unchanged, still combed
by kites and swifts, the homing rooks.
There, summer months will always turn
to heather, purple deep as grief.
Where the hollow-way cuts through,
follow uphill over brook, pasture, wood,
search for a stone. It may be bedded in
but when you find it, run your fingers
over chiselled words that speak
to a future left behind, a navigation note
of crow-flight, water-flow, satellite and star,
which carves the plan for going home.
A useful hulk of stone, for gatepost, step,
a threshold. That stone, those words
through gritted teeth, that's where I am.

October 4ᵗʰ 2007

Through that long night I paced, stared at the stars
and wished with every breath, that you'd be safe.
Then morning came, and on the phone, your voice.
Listen, you said. I heard his tiny sounds and my heart
leapt for you. And when I rushed the morning miles
it was to see you safe, my lovely girl, my first-born,
and I wanted so to mother you. *Look at him*, you said.
And then I saw you whole, complete, child in your arms,
and knew that this is what you grew up for,
the biggest step beyond me, and I loved you more.

What I've Learned

Those ants in line
          that follow me in
                    from the pristine forest
          and march onto my page
are not required first to wipe their feet.

Plastic Bag and a Railway Ticket
for E.J.

Oxford's nothing left for me. The cafe
where I used to write all day (toasted teacake,
pot of tea) is fast food now, the council flat
they gave me, far too loud and dangerous,
but dear John G's five thousand pounds
will take me far. I don't need much,
a book or two, a change of clothes,
my sonnets – I've paper-clipped them
all together in this Asda bag,
and when I reach my destination, then
I'll leave them on the seat and go.
Where that will be I'm not quite sure,
but maybe Italy or Spain. I'll be careful
of the gap between the platform and the train.

Dandelions

for Lucas

Chrome-yellow suns, their quick turn
into misty spheres. Here at the playground
where he loves the swings, the climbing frame,
the long slide built into the slope of the field,
I pick a clock and blow the down. Then him,
his perfect lips, wet and shushing, seeds
stuck to his mouth, the tickle on his nose,
the little parachutes adrift he tries to catch
like bubbles, he says – another, and again.

I don't explain the game, how many blows
to tell the time, his pleasure's in the drift
and spread of cloudy tufts. Nor do I count,
but hold this moment fixed against the rush,
his certain speed – boy, then youth, then man.
It will be quick, will time me out. Dandelion
weed, the stain of stem-milk for warts,
pee-the-beds, the greying wisps of hair
released with one short breath into the air.

End

I want the scissors to be sharp,
the cut decisive, clean.
There will be music playing
to distract the others waiting
so the moment's mine.
Or better, I will be looking out to sea
as the whetstone's at the blades,
I'll be musicking the waves
with sand between my toes and I'll stoop
to pick a perfect shell and hold it to my ear
or better even still, I'll be dancing
in a corner of a dim-lit room
about to say – so, shall we go ...
when snip, simple as that
and nothing more

Index of Titles

Lightning Source UK Ltd.
Milton Keynes UK
UKOW04f0935020915

257935UK00002B/61/P